Be Magnificent

My Path to Empowerment & Joy

Christine Quinn

Disclaimer: This is my story from my personal experiences. I share what works for me. Please do your own research and consult your own body or outside experts to determine what works for you. Thank You.

Dedication

To Ada, Carol, Dianna Magic and Fernanda….from the beginning

Table of Contents

What does it mean to be a Magnificent Woman? To experience the tiniest glimpse of divinity, the merest hint of infinite promise?

You are reading this book because—in your soul—you believe there is more to life than what you can see or touch. You are reading this for a reason. You know there is a deeper way to communicate and connect with the world and the people around you. Let this book speak to your soul.

Magnificent

The word "Magnificent" itself conjures up images of greatness and dignity. Synonyms found in a dictionary include "splendid, spectacular, impressive, striking, glorious", all words that send shivers down the spine. This Middle English word, via Old French, is sourced from the Latin, meaning: making great, serving to magnify, all based on being "great". There may be a link to Old Norse as a synonym for "powerhouse". Not bad at all. To embark on a journey to Magnificence already has a history from multiple cultures throughout history. Sounds like a terrific type of person to be!

This is about letting our inner confidence shine outward. It is about holding our heads high and facing the rest of the world eye-to-eye and knowing so deeply and truly who we really are—that joy is overflowing.

So, who is this Magnificent Woman? In truth, any and all of us are magnificent. We hold it within ourselves to walk in dignity, dance in joy and choose to be remarkably happy. We need to remember who we are internally and wake up to the knowledge that our souls are infinite. We need to believe that who we are right now, this instant, makes a difference in the world. We have to listen to the full truth and tune out the little lies and self-defeating phrases we hear on a daily basis. We cannot focus on other factors: a painful past, a destructive relationship, not enough support, not enough money, not enough of anything else. We have to look at the here and now and claim this Magnificence by realizing the power of that word and believing in ourselves. Nice words, sure. But how do we really begin to put these words into life-changing actions? After all, thoughts become actions (behaviors) don't they? And behaviors change our thoughts, and on & on.

Various cultures and religions throughout history have focused on the power of the spoken word and how believing and repeating certain phrases and mantras can bring these words into our very spirit and take on life. Authors, philosophers and religious leaders teach affirmations and bring these phrases into the common cultural awareness, bringing hundreds of thousands of people together to chant, pray or shout out power words that actually become part of the general vernacular. Even today, experts in marketing and advertising positions know the truth of this: the more words are repeated and embraced, the more they are believed to be true.

Why Do I Believe All This?

Magnificence is about waking up with joy. It's about choosing to be happy. It's about acknowledging your body as being strong and fabulous. It's about looking in the mirror and smiling and saying, "I am so pleased to be me today." It's about sharing these thoughts with people, either as a life coach or a hypnotherapist or a friend or a seminar leader. It's about sharing the excitement, the enthusiasm, and the exuberance of being an accepted woman. Knowing that you don't have to doubt yourself. If the claim of "Magnificence" causes you to blush or shy away, then please keep reading.

For me, I don't second guess the details of my looks or if what I'm wearing is top fashion or if my makeup is impeccable—none of those things matter when your soul is rich and full. In talking to others, I've watched women who haven't heard about this way of magnificence, how their eyes light up when they begin to lean into the conversation, drinking it all in, it made me realize that this is not something that's just simply a 'given' or to be taken for granted. In case this is a new concept for you too, please know that this attitude is about choosing to be magnificent, choosing to be delighted with life, choosing to inhale as well as exhale, choosing to move with your own rhythm, your own beat of your own big, beautiful drum—but without judgment, without remorse, without regret, without shame. And I grew up with a lot of shame.

It's like living in light. I don't mean that frivolously. I mean, it really is being enlightened. Nothing is so perfect in my life that it can't use some input or some improvement eventually, but for today, right now, I choose to feel terrific. I am terrific. I believe that when you feel good, you look good. Oddly enough, this is the exact opposite of what we are told culturally, by sellers of beauty products and fashion stylists. We continuously see advertisements claiming that longer lashes or firmer skin will make us more attractive. That more “this” or less “that” is all we need to be pleasing to the outside world. We don’t have to appear to look appealing to someone else’s definition of “good” – the truth is that when we feel good we look fabulous.

This all comes from inside. I believe my spirit is healthy and thriving. That's what it means to be magnificent. That's what it means to be passionate about being magnificent. Even if it brings you to tears to learn about it and to actually believe that we can all be this way, we’ve got each other for support. We've got each other for encouragement. We believe in each other. This is the power of true friendship, a circle of support, a circle of community and when you share this, we only get stronger. We get more confident. We get continuously more assured of ourselves.

I believe I am a Magnificent Woman. This is something I know and carry deep in my soul. There is no doubt. How can I possibly be so sure? I didn’t start out this way. I grew up in a dirty, crowded city in a middle-class fundamentally religious family. We were always pinching pennies and never seemed to have enough of anything. I was third in line for the hand-me-downs in school and nothing ever fit quite right. I always appeared slightly disheveled or sloppy in stretched-out, ill-fitting clothing with mismatched buttons that had been sewn on numerous times. There was a continuous feeling of shame about never quite "looking good", it didn't matter if I were at home or at school – the impression was that I couldn't fit in. Home life was tense, there was always a quiver of anger or resentment in the air. My Dad had two words he continuously used to describe his children: rotten & miserable. As every adult now understands, unfortunately, negative words carry just as much power in our souls as do positive affirmations. Even at mandatory church attendance several times a week we were subject to this abusive verbal (and later physical) mistreatment. From Junior High School until HS graduation, I was at best a wallflower, somehow invisible. My tragic uniform in life seemed to be bad skin, bad eyes and bad teeth. I don't think I found much joy in being female, only humiliation. It took me years of reading everything I could find, listening to teachers and thought leaders and attending empowerment seminars before I could give myself permission to believe there could ever be something "**greater**".

Then I had an epiphany. The online dictionary defines this experience as a sudden, intuitive perception of or insight into the reality or essential meaning of something. Just as when the mathematician Archimedes shouted "Eureka" or Newton watched an apple drop straight down from the tree. This certainly helps explain it. Quicker than the blink of an eye, so fast I had no words to describe the time, I changed. I remember I was outside walking somewhere and had the impression that the earth might have stood still. I can't remember if I lost balance because it all seemed so fast, and then it was over. But I came away *changed*. I knew my Spirit had shifted. I felt as if I were made of light. For that fraction of a fraction of a second, I understood Magnificence. Every Goddess archetype I had ever studied began to jockey for expression. I felt the grace of Venus, the might of Durga, the joy of Hathor, the light of Astarte, the pride of Isis and the complete and total comprehension of the Earth Goddess Gaia. I had touched the Divine. I knew that I knew I was different, and not simply different but better, grander, greater than I had ever imagined possible. This knowledge was so deep and so sure that I didn't even think to question it. It was glorious! Better yet, I was glorious!

This is the beginning of the truth I want to share. We ALL have access to this incredible experience. My desire for every woman I meet is to touch that spark of Divine Femininity that resides within. To be able to walk past a mirror and gasp out loud at the incredible sight before you. To delightfully celebrate every cell, every inch and every curve of your delightful sacred temple.

PART I

We all know what this Magnificence is not. It is not about our outward appearance. So much of what we see and hear (and are expected to accept) about female attractiveness has nothing to do with "us" or about who we really are. It is certainly not about being ashamed of having a less than perfect airbrushed body. Who defines desirability in the female form? Does an artist or poet determine the parameters of beauty? A brief look at art through the ages shows that appearances, and cultural standards of beauty, change significantly through time. The concept of an attractive, desirable female has changed drastically throughout history. Traditionally the ability to bear and raise children was the most evolutionary important trait a woman displayed. Think of the archeological excavations that have dug up countless statues of the female form with the focus entirely on the birth canal. The "Sheela-na-Gig" figurines from the British Isles and ancient Ireland are carvings of naked women displaying an exaggerated vulva.

The emphasis was entirely on the female anatomy and the ability to bring new life into the world. New life through birth was celebrated as natural, powerful and perhaps sacred. These figurines have been found in hundreds of holy wells, ancient stone structures and towers. There is no sense of shame or need to hide the female body. It is celebrated for its sexuality and life affirming capability.

Findings of Marija Gimbultas, PhD

Dr. Marija Gimbultas (1921-1994) was a professor of European Archaeology at the University of Californian and Curator of Old-World Archaeology at UCLA Museum of Cultural History. An author of more than twenty scholarly books, she wrote *"The Goddesses & Gods of Old Europe"*, and *"The Language of the Goddess"*. Her research was extensive: she spoke seven languages and read an additional seventeen. In her studies and interpretation of thousands of symbolic artifacts from early Neolithic ("New Stone Age") villages from around 7000 to 35000 BCE she established many main themes of religious worship of both the Universe and the living body of the Goddess-Mother-Creator. Often compared with the groundbreaking work deciphering of the Rosetta Stone in the early 1800's, Gimbultas' work assembled, classified and interpreted some two thousand symbols from the early Neolithic village sites of Europe. She was able to prepare a fundamental glossary of symbolic motifs as keys to the mythology and folklore of that era. She deciphered these signs, symbols and artifacts to be associated with the main religion of the time as understanding the Universe through the living body of the Goddess – Mother – Creator. Dr. Gimbultas believed she uncovered proof of an ancient Goddess oriented civilization that lived peacefully in harmony with Nature and enjoyed a high degree of economic, social and sexual equality. Many of the sites she excavated date back more than 8000 years BCE and reveal much about the social and spiritual practices of the people who lived there. The deities worshipped were overwhelmingly female and depicted the focus on reproduction and a reverence for Nature. Carvings of the Goddess were found in caves, temples, tree trunks, and buried in the crop fields. The artifacts discovered lacked images of warfare and male anatomy or domination. While not supposing a complete Matriarchal Society, it does suggest the theory that equality and shared responsibility for the raising and safety of the tribe was considered normal at this point in time.

Dr. Gimbultas was highly criticized by her (male) peers for her theories of a peaceful and matriarchal (female led) era predating the Indo-European "Bronze Age." The idea of harmony between the sexes, combined with a reverence for Mother Nature was considered closer to mythology than archeology. Yet the abundance of the Goddess figurines and shrines found in numerous geographical locations begs for an explanation. Before the obsession of war and conquest, how did we live? How did we worship? How did we celebrate?

The Divine Feminine – The Goddess Archetype

We live in a world of symbols, patterns, ideas and metaphors. The renowned Swiss psychiatrist and founder of analytical psychology Carl Jung (1875-1961), who believed in “emotionally charged associations” and helped define human personalities, defined **Archetypes** as universal, primal symbols and images that derive from the collective unconscious. These prototypes would be used in myths and storytelling across different cultures to explain and understand human behavior. Jung sorted these types into areas that would provide structure, leave a mark, connect to others or experience the spiritual journey as their purpose in the community.

We can see the **Goddess Archetype** in all of these areas. The Goddess is an acknowledged and understood archetype that embodies wisdom, nurturing, guidance, grace, might, strength, sensuality and power. For centuries people would continue to celebrate the power of the Divine Feminine in their worship of the Goddess. Even today She is worshipped as the Lady, or even the Mother of God. The Goddess represented the Earth & the Sky, the Divine Mother and the Wise Healer. Today we can choose to take on the characteristics of any Goddess from any pantheon (collective) in order to charge up our own personal energy, change our perspective or even discover a deeper sense of our own divinity within ourselves.

Eons before the northern Indo-European war tribes rode south with their weapons and their war gods, peaceful peoples cultivated the land and worshipped some form of a Mother Goddess. This Goddess figure was synonymous with the land, the provider and the nurturer. Different variations of the Mother Goddess in ancient cultures also depicted her as the Almighty Queen, the Warrior, the Protector and the Eternal Giver of Light. We can find these Archetypes in every corner of the World.

We look to Goddess archetypes to try to recognize what stirs within us, how we experience our emotions and search for meaning and authenticity. Perhaps we see a glimpse of our incredible potential when we see how we can respond to various challenges and opportunities – with inner strength, wisdom, grace, compassion, delight, ferocity or a combination of all of those and more. The point is that it is our choice: we decide how to confront the day and who exactly we desire to be. When we need to "pull on power" or "breathe in charity" or take any kind of action that requires focus and mindfulness, perhaps we are looking at a Goddess Archetype that fits the moment.

Hera - Dignity

Let's start with Hera, the Queen of the Celestial Skies to the ancient Greeks and surrounding islands. Hera, the original Queen of the Gods represented Power, Dignity, Control and Feminism. Dignity is defined as "a sense of pride, of self-respect" and also as "the quality or state of being worthy, honored, or esteemed." I like to call on Hera when I find myself needing to access some poise in my life and when I need to straighten my spine and hold my head up high.

Approximately 300 years before the invasion of the northern invaders and their powerful warrior Sky God, the Greek culture honored the "Queen" they called Hera. Temples were built in her honor and women would come to dance, to sing and to burn offerings in exchange for inner strength, abundant crops and a healthy & happy life. She was depicted as a majestic figure, adorned with a high cylindrical polos crown as she moved among her followers.

Long before the followers of Zeus entered Greece, the people there honored her as their own chief divinity. She was their Celestial Queen and ancestral Mother and she ruled alone, without a consort. Hera represented the epitome of woman's strength and power. Symbolizing the inner essence of feminine development, women came to her temple at every stage of their lives.

As the mythology evolved, the Sky God became known as Zeus, the Almighty. The mighty Sky God wanted to own the Queen of Heaven, so naturally Zeus wanted Hera. He took on divine, human and animal personas, then revealed himself and proceeded to rape her for 300 years. This is a direct correlation to the officials of the city-states explaining how the new Olympian Sky God was invincible and graciously took Hera as wife. The adherents of the temple of Hera were now folded into the cult of Zeus as "King" of all gods. The reason Hera was accorded a status of a goddess (note the lower case "g") and not neglected completely was to "integrate her cult" with the one that worshipped Zeus.

Through myth and literature, Hera became the goddess of marriage. Under her sign and through her control, the act of marriage "tamed" men to great advantage for the Greek State. The State in turn extended honors to her cult and supported her temples because in parts of Greece men could not be recognized as citizens until the day of their marriage, So these men who worshipped could then marry, become citizens and continue to provide the city-state with a ready supply of laborers, taxes and military personnel to boot. The government got their army laborers, and allowed the worship of Hera to continue in a role now relegated to that of a jealous, embittered wife.

At this time, marriage belonged to the State. It belonged completely to Society, to the Community. Zeus and Hera represented social stability; they *are* the state in essence. All living in the area could be married by a representative of the state or a Justice of the Peace at their City Hall, since marriage was a secular event. The tax coders and all inheritance laws acknowledge that a fundamental structure of the organization of society is marriage. It is a fundamental structure of society belonging to the polis or the city or the community.

How did mythology try to change Hera into a negative and jealous goddess?

One way was that it exerted the power of the worshippers of Zeus over the worshippers of Goddess Hera. By portraying her negatively and diminishing her powers through myths and legends, the influence held by her cult was also significantly reduced and eventually, the role of Hera as a powerful and independent Goddess was forgotten.

The other reason is that when a society worships a female deity as the sole goddess without attaching her to a male god, it shows traces of a non-patriarchal social order. The portrayal of the pillar of this world negatively shows a shift from a non-patriarchal society to an increasingly authoritarian one. The question of who benefits by these myths and the negative representation of Goddess Hera, the answer would be an increasingly stratified society trying to drown the voices of powerful female figures. All worship would be directed toward a mandatory organized religion, determined by the elders of the city.

So, contrary to the popular perceptions, Hera is not a "bad" goddess. Her negative portrayal is an outcome of vested interests and the rise of a Sky God war focused society and if you look hard enough, in Hera you can find residual traces of a peaceful mother Goddess social order. So, while mythology books and encyclopedias continue to refer to Hera as the bitter jealous and vindictive wife of the cheating Zeus, I prefer to channel her incredible dignity and self-esteem whenever I remember every incident I was ridiculed, passed over, ignored or bullied.

My head is as high as the original Celestial Goddess herself.

Hathor - Joy

Another timeless favorite popular Goddess is the Egyptian Hathor. She is the Ultimate Rebel, Self-Crowned Queen of all Worlds, the Sovereign One. Hathor shows us how to become liberated, to access our self-definition, and live by our own rules. She shows us how to re-crown ourselves Serpent-Queen (to shed old ways and grow new life), Goddess most Beloved. I like to emulate the persona of Hathor when I want to enjoy Romance for the sheer joy of it, when I want to celebrate all the graciousness of femininity without the arrogance mythically associated with Aphrodite or Venus. This is complete and total indulgence.

In her role as goddess of joy, pleasure, fertility, and all things feminine, Hathor was one of the most important goddesses in ancient Egypt and popular among royalty and common people alike. She was worshiped for over several thousand years, from the early years of the ancient Egyptian religion (c. 4000 BCE) until its end (c. 500 CE). Myth also has it that Hathor was a sky goddess together with NUT. They were the sisters associated with the Milky Way, which was seen as the milk flowing from the udders of a heavenly cow. Hathor's character centered on femininity, but although she had power over women's issues such as fertility, beauty, childbirth, and love, she was also worshipped by men and had many male priests. Among others, she was celebrated as the Mistress of Life.

While other Goddesses represented wealth, fertility and power, Hathor brought the sweetest gift: love. She is intimately connected with our dearest pleasure and joys. Songs celebrating joy, longing, sensuality and delight were offered up to this Goddess. Three thousand years later these songs are considered some of the world's finest poetry. One of the most popular, and longest-lasting, of the Egyptian goddesses, Hathor was mentioned as early around 2890 BCE, far before the entry into the Nile valley of such foreign gods as sun-god Ra.

Since she survived for so long, Hathor took on a number of roles, including spells as the goddess of love, beauty, dance, and music. Her name was invoked to bring love and affection into one's life. She was also considered the Goddess of beginnings – including infatuation – which marked the beginning of love.

She was called the Lady of Love, the Golden One and Queen of the Dance. Dancing was one of her primary forms of worship. Due to the amount of Joy the dancing brought, music itself fell under Hathor's dominion. As the Golden One, her followers acknowledged both her solar identity and the golden light of Love.

In this same era, in other geographical regions, the Supreme Goddess of Life, Fertility and Power reigned unmatched. In ancient Sumeria this Goddess of sensuality and love and was known as Inanna, in Phoenicia she was Astarte. The Hittites called her Sauska and throughout Mesopotamian regions she was Ishtar. In all origin stories she stood powerful and alone, without a required consort. Only later, as the conquering tribes took control with their male war gods and created history, did the joy of romance and sensuality devolve into shame and submission. When we choose to emulate a Goddess today, we can choose the original Hathor: she of song, dance, romance and pleasure.

The desire for love and affection is a powerful human drive, even compared with hunger or thirst. Like the basic level in the hierarchy of needs, the comfort of love is likened to a warm blanket against the world's cold darkness.

Hathor is the goddess of infatuation – when the lover's every movement appear charming, when joy erupts from every encounter and even a ray of sunlight seems effervescent. Regardless of age, this is a happy time, a time of hope and complete delight. In all things, Hathor's domain is Happiness. This is also our choice to make at any time we desire. Why not choose joy? Who wouldn't want to embrace delight? We can choose this any time, any place, and any way and at any age. . It is truly, simply up to us. This is just another part of being a magnificent woman, on an everyday basis.

Minerva - Wisdom

Another Goddess archetype worth examining is the Goddess of Wisdom and Knowledge. The Romans called her Minerva, although the origin of this worship was thought to be Etruscan, which predated the Roman civilization in the same region.

The Greeks favored Athena, she of wisdom and peace. Later this deity was transformed into the leader of War who came into being by means of bursting out of the "thigh" (What could that possibly symbolize?), which was later changed to the skull of Zeus. To the Greeks, Wisdom couldn't even be born of a woman. In Celtic mythology, Danu was the goddess of wisdom, intellect, inspiration, fertility, and wind. Her name stems from the ancient Irish word dan, meaning poetry, wisdom, knowledge, art, and skill.

Saraswati is the Hindu goddess of wisdom, creativity, intellect, and learning. She's also considered a source of inspiration for different arts, including poetry, music, drama, and also science. Her name stems from two Sanskrit words – Sara, meaning essence, and Swa, which means oneself. Therefore, the goddess represents the essence or spirit of oneself. I want to list all these different aspects of the Wisdom Goddess to emphasize how ancient the belief is that the female deity encompassed the mind: the seat of the intellect and the home of the Spirit. For eons these female characteristics have been highly revered and represent true empowerment, which is ours today.

Let's briefly go back to Minerva. She was one of the most powerful gods in the entire pantheon. The public religion of ancient Rome consisted of a powerful triad comprised of Jupiter, Juno, and Minerva.

Today, statues of Minerva can often be found in schools and libraries. Even though it's been thousands of years since the Romans worshiped her, Minerva continues to stand for wisdom and the act of creating things. By a process of folk etymology, the Romans could have linked her foreign name to the root *men-* in Latin words such as ***mens*** meaning "mind", perhaps because one of her aspects as goddess pertained to the intellectual.

Once held in high esteem as the Goddess of Wisdom and Peace, the warriors from the Northern Steppes changed her story to be born only from the Patriarch (no life-giving mother figure) from the head or directly from the thigh (genitals) as the Goddess of War. The invaders eventually took away the stubborn power of the Goddess by denying women basic rights including the right to vote (which the US didn't even grant until 1920.)

She is known as the Patron Goddess of Medicine and Knowledge. She was the virgin goddess (only meaning not yoked to a man, nothing to do with the physical breaking of the skin of the hymen) of music, medicine, wisdom, commerce, and the crafts. She is often depicted with her sacred creature, an owl usually named as the "owl of Minerva", which symbolized her association with wisdom and knowledge. The owl suggests Minerva's power is so strong that she chooses her actions with consideration and knowledge.

Like Athena and Medusa (and Hathor the Serpent Queen), Minerva was often also symbolized by the snake. Snakes shed their skin, representing a new stage of life. They also held a protective role in the home by being placed in the grain house to protect the crops and devour rodents and pests and were held in the highest regard. The snake became "evil" in contemporary western culture by being associated with the Goddess (the original Eve) and the fruit or the "apple". Freud fed into this deceit by associating the snake with male genitalia. Clearly, great care was taken to ensure that associating the Female with wisdom was someone to be feared.

Lakshmi - Abundance

Many women feel a sense of embarrassment or uneasiness with the idea of abundance. It seems to be associated with greed, ostentation and a shallow personality. The idea of a powerful female living a life of wealth and abundance is a fearful image to many even today. In the age of the patriarchy, women found their wealth and their very sustenance at the mercy or the whim of the strong male. Not that long ago, when women were finally admitted to Universities to pursue higher education it became socially acceptable to be lauded for achieving an "MRS" degree. Why is there such a taboo concerning a female and wealth?

The practice of personifying the beauty and bounty of the earth as a Goddess was prevalent in all ancient cultures. This celebration of abundance predates the idea that only the patriarch could provide all sustenance. It is as old as our collective memory.

The Greeks had Core, the corn-goddess. The Romans called her Demeter, Goddess of the Earth and all producing fruits, thus ruling over the art of agriculture. In Egypt the Mother of all Abundance was Isis, in Persia she was Anahita and the Norse worshipped her as Freia. Shri-Lakshmi is the Hindu form of the timeless mother-goddess who nurtures and nourishes all life. Let's focus a bit on Lakshmi, for she is indeed abundance personified.

The Goddess Lakshmi is referred to as the goddess of fortune and pleasure. She is a goddess born with and personified by a diverse range of talents and powers. Lakshmi means fortune, prosperity, wealth, good luck, success, accomplishment, beauty, grace, charm, loveliness, splendor, luster, sovereign power, auspiciousness and so on. Goddess Lakshmi represents all these qualities. Her other popular name ***Siri*** denotes wealth, which in the ancient times around the world was represented by the wealth of food grains. Cascades of gold coins are often seen flowing from her hands, suggesting that those who worship her will gain wealth. The goddess symbolizes not only material wealth but also the wealth of all kinds from food to fame and the richness of life. Hence, she has many aspects representing various forms of wealth, richness, abundance, perfection, fullness and enjoyment.

However, wealth does not come by itself.

Knowledge is the basis of wealth and enjoyment. Besides, wealth and knowledge, one also celebrated family. Hence, the three eternal aspects of Mother Goddess, knowledge, wealth and procreation, carry a lot of importance in Hindu way of life. Lakshmi not only represents material wealth but wealth of all kinds. She is also worshipped for abundance in courage, knowledge, strength and victory.

There should be nothing stopping us from declaring abundance and prosperity as our right in whatever area of our life we choose. It can be gold coins, ears of corn or handfuls of rich soil as long as we put our "wealth" to work in our lives.

Quan Yin - Compassion

It is fascinating to learn that many of the ancient pantheons had no place for a deity to represent compassion or mercy. The focus instead was on power or profit, and the concept of compassion could be perceived as a weakness. Leniency could be granted by the judges or the courts, but it would come with a cost. Yet one of the strengths of the powerful Goddess is her compassion and ability to empathize, or feel another's pain.

For over a thousand years, in China, Japan and Korea, Quan Yin has been revered as the Goddess of compassion. This Crone Goddess archetype is most often associated with kindness, gentleness and helpfulness who epitomizes the One who can give of herself to those in need. She provides the experience of generosity, encouraging care and concern for others and putting self-centered concerns aside. Compassion is not co-dependency. The ability to understand another person's pain or emotional turmoil is not the same as supporting or reliving it. It is loving and caring but separate.

Psychologically and spiritually, there is a connection between physical & emotional healing, compassion and mercy. Men, women and children suffering from invisible illnesses have called upon an all-powerful force or all "merciful" Goddess for healing and deliverance from every corner of the world. Today we can choose to be exceedingly healthy and shamelessly kind and compassionate.

Kali - Protector

Every culture has a Goddess who was able to cause havoc, display great feats of formidable strength and fight and crush evil doers. This archetype shows up for us today when we are resilient, independent and the maker of our own destiny. The Romans had Hecate, the Patroness and Protector of magic and holder of the Keys. Sekhmet was worshipped and feared in Egypt as the

"Powerful, Terrible One" who controlled fire, destruction, war and authority. Her followers called on her and fled to her temple when under any type of physical or psychic attack. In the Norse pantheon, the cruel Hel rules over the kingdom of the dead and leads its army in battle. Warriors who die honorably are protected from her wrath, those who do not suffer without mercy.

The Mayan Crone Goddess Ixchel was an earth and a war goddess. She was the "giver of children" as the personification of the Midwife. Depicted as an elderly shamanic woman with jaguar ears and a pale white or bright red face, she wears a skirt marked with bones and symbols of divination. While one face is turned toward life and birth, the other is to death and destruction. She was the protector of fertility and procreation and known by the symbol of the crescent moon. A twisted serpent serves as her headdress and she is often drawn with the claws of the jaguar instead of human feet, reinforcing her connection with the

Earth. Though protective of young mothers, she continues to carry a sword and spear to be seen as a fierce warrior. Ixchel terrorizes those who cross her path without her permission or who dare to mean harm to the ones in her care.

The most ferocious of all is Kali, the fierce form of the Hindu Goddess Durga. Master of death, time and change, Kali is associated with sexuality and violence and still considered a strong Mother figure. She embodies "shakti"-feminine energy, sexuality, creativity and fertility. Kali is a Goddess dark of mind, body and soul, fearsome in death and destruction. She doesn't fit easily into the category of good or evil because she transcends both. Some teachings consider her to be a force of nature, or more specifically, a "force of time". In this sense she existed before the Universe began and will continue after the Universe ends. So any limitations of the physical plane do not apply. She is a symbol of the Divine Mother Nature: elemental, creative, nurturing and devouring in turns. Her image reflects her duality. She is often depicted as the slayer of demons (the enemy) with multiple arms and legs each holding symbols of victory. Kali wears a skirt of human arms and a necklace of decapitated heads, symbolizing the victory of suffering and death. She dances on one foot holding the necklace of the defeated and a crown of gold on her head.

There is nothing shy or retiring about the Goddess Protector. She is the conqueror, the defender of the underdog and takes no prisoners to accomplish her goals. Not a bad archetype to have in your arsenal.

All of Us Each of Us

We have just looked at a handful of historical and cultural examples of archetypes and qualities. The Goddess Archetype is something that is a part of us. It is up to each of us to choose how to express ourselves spiritually and connect with the divine feminine – every minute of every day. We choose what we need. See what fits, try it on. Try another.

This is our honor and our right.

This is our choice.

PART 2

The Incredible Mind

Our brain is the most complex part of the human body. This three-pound organ is composed of the brainstem, the cerebellum and the cerebrum. It controls all functions of our body, interpreting information from the outside world and carrying the very essence of who we are: our mind and soul. It is more powerful than any computer and uses approximately twenty percent of the body's energy at any given time. It controls what we think and what we feel, how we learn and remember, and the way we move and talk.

So how do we keep it as healthy and happy as possible? We want it to function in "tip-top" shape to provide the best level of activity we can have at every stage of our life.

Such a powerful organ may at first seem overwhelming in its scope and capability. Scientists have been both fascinated and baffled by every new discovery of what makes our brains work. The great news is that we can take an active part in keeping our brains healthy, in ensuring the mind-body connection stays strong. Through foods, herbs, physical activities, sounds and words we make conscious decisions to have magnificent, incredible minds.

The brain itself is divided into two hemispheres, or two separate halves. Each half controls or manages certain functions. There is no "good or bad" since we require both working together to survive. The theory is that people are either left-brained or right-brained, meaning that one side of their brain is dominant. The quick synopsis is that the left brain is more analytical, logical, verbal and methodical. It helps us with facts, thinking in words, reading and writing. The right brain (the other side) is the part that pushes our imagination, our intuition and holistic thinking. It has a more creative way of thinking with nonverbal cues.

For a moment, think of your brain like a muscle. To keep it fit, you can develop a set of exercises to stimulate one hemisphere or the other. By activating the left side of your brain, you will strengthen your ability to analyze words and numbers. Since the left side of your brain processes language and mathematics, puzzles or games in these subjects help sharpen this hemisphere. When you try to solve a word puzzle, electrical and chemical impulses travel among the neurons in the left hemisphere until you identify the answer. Crossword puzzles, Sudoku and any challenging word games keep your memory sharp and your mind learning.

The right side of the brain is creative and artistic. Activating the right brain through mental stimulation and activities has been shown to increase vitality and potentially grow new brain cells. Drawing and painting help you explore your creative side. Try using your non dominant hand to draw a picture. Then try it again. Another exercise to try is breathing through one nostril at a time. When breathing through the left nostril, it helps to improve the function of the right hemisphere of the brain. Just five minutes of Alternate Nostril Breathing every morning, prior to taking an examination or before a social event, can help open the door to gain access to your entire brain. Increasing oxygen to the brain reduces the brain bound free radicals, improving memory and cognition. Alternate Nostril Breathing has the immediate advantages of increasing mental sharpness. (This is known as the yogic practice of Nadi Shodhana)

What we put into our body affects our general overall health. This is just as true for our brain as it is for any other area of our body. What we put in impacts our energy levels, our mental clarity, our memory and our ability to handle stress.

Let's start with the foods we eat. This may all sound like repetitive information that you have seen again and again everywhere you turn. If so, good for you. If not, consider this a reminder of what your brain is calling out for and telling you to add to your regular intake. We tend to rely on convenience foods and forget what the inner machine needs to use for fuel to “Live Well”.

All living organisms use oxygen to metabolize and use dietary nutrients to produce energy for survival. Oxidative stress is an imbalance between free radicals and antioxidants in your body. Free radicals form that are capable of attacking the healthy cells of the body. Putting foods rich in antioxidants is especially important for brain health, as our brains are highly susceptible to oxidative stress, which can contribute to age-related cognitive decline and brain diseases.

Antioxidants can be broken down into two groups: Flavonoids found in plants, and non-flavonoids found in minerals, plant pigments and vitamins.

Plant foods that are considered power food for the brain are easily accessible and can be added to your everyday diet. There are some readily available examples in your kitchen today.

Blueberries

This fruit contains a compound that has anti-inflammatory and antioxidant effects. This means blueberries can shrink internal inflammation which reduces the risk of brain aging and neurodegenerative disease.

The anthocyanins and other antioxidants in blueberries and pomegranates have been linked to increased nerve signaling in the brain, improved memory as well as more efficient removal of excess glucose (sugar) in the brain, which leads to more balanced brain energy.

Grapes

Research has shown that grape juice can help reduce oxidative stress and improve memory. Resveratrol, a naturally occurring highly powerful antioxidant is most prominent in natural grape juice and red wine. It contains protective qualities that can help your body with daily functions and fight off illnesses. Most notably, resveratrol helps with brain and heart inflammation by providing a protective lining for your blood vessels and preventing injury. So, hooray for red wine!

Walnuts

Not only does it look like a brain, but the walnut is considered a powerful supplement for your mind. They have a significantly high concentration of DHA, a type of Omega-3 fatty acid. This is the same ingredient we find in consuming fatty fish (salmon, sardines and mackerel). Among other things, DHA has been shown to protect brain health in newborns, improve cognitive performance in adults, and prevent or upgrade age-related cognitive decline. One study even shows that expectant mothers who get enough DHA have smarter kids.

Dark Chocolate

Some of the happiest research I ever read indicates that dark chocolate may improve the function of the brain. It has shown significant improvement in cognitive function in older adults and improved blood flow to the brain. It may improve verbal fluency and several risk factors for disease, as well. There is considerable evidence that cocoa can provide powerful health benefits, being especially protective against heart disease. Dark chocolate boosts the production of feel-good chemicals called endorphins.

Endorphins bind with opiate receptors in the brain leading to feelings of euphoria, like the kind joggers get from "runner's high." They also reduce pain and diminish the negative effects of stress. Chocolate is a good source of tryptophan, an amino acid precursor to serotonin, the neurotransmitter of happiness and positive mood. Chocolate is the main food source of anandamide, a naturally occurring compound called the "bliss molecule." This is some of the best research I have ever discovered!

Vitamins

Non flavonoid antioxidant sources can be found in Vitamin C and E, minerals, and plant pigments. Vitamin C is found in nutrient dense citrus fruits such as oranges, limes, tangerines and grapefruit and other fruits such as guavas, chili peppers, Kakadu plums and cherries. Vitamin E is a group of powerful antioxidants studied for their ability to help your body ward off infections, improve skin health and generally protect cells throughout your entire body. You can add Vitamin E to your diet by including avocado, mango and pumpkin to ensure your brain is getting enough of this preventive aid.

Nutrients

An amazing and rarely heard of nutrient that is vital to our brain is selenium. It is an essential mineral and can **only be obtained**

through your diet. We only need small amounts, but it plays a big role in some important processes, including our metabolism and thyroid function. As an antioxidant, it helps defend the body against chronic conditions like heart disease or some forms of cancer. Some research studies have shown selenium can reduce DNA damage and boost the immune system. Lower blood levels of selenium have been linked with memory loss and diseases affecting cognitive behavior. Selenium is important for the proper functioning of your thyroid gland. In fact, thyroid tissue contains a higher amount of selenium than any other organ in the human body. This powerful mineral can help protect the thyroid against oxidation damage and plays an important role in the production of thyroid hormones. Healthy glands are important. The thyroid gland regulates your metabolism and controls growth. You can find selenium in many healthy foods that are readily available. Look for seasonal oysters, yellow-fin tuna, halibut, sunflower seeds or Brazil nuts. As with all plant-based food, the amount of minerals will vary depending on the quality content of the soil where the produce is grown so do your research.

Antioxidants

For antioxidant sources found in plant pigments, look to the rainbow! Carotenoids are the orange pigments found in foods such as pumpkin, carrot and sweet potato. Beta-carotene is a precursor to Vitamin A. Lutein is found in dark green vegetables such as kale, broccoli, kiwi, and spinach. Lutein is best known for being a nutrient that benefits the eyes and can be found in bell peppers and parsley. Lycopene is the red pigment found in tomatoes, pink grapefruit and watermelon.

We decide what we put into our bodies; we decide what we put into our brains. Knowing this, why wouldn't we make wise decisions when given the opportunity?

Automatic Functions

Something I have only recently learned about is referred to as The Brain Derived Neurotrophic Factor. Some researchers describe BDNF as a kind of "aftercare" for your brain, helping your neurons heal and create new connections after surviving the daily grind. The name comes from the Greek neuro for "nerve" and trophis "pertaining to food, nourishment or growth." For ages people have expected and accepted the idea that brain shrinkage and memory loss occurred with age. Dr. Christiane Northrup, author of "Women's Bodies, Women's Wisdom" and "Goddesses Never Age" shows another approach. While some MRI scans on patients over time show that an area of the brain called the hippocampus (the part of the brain that is involved in emotions, learning, and memory formation) may get smaller with age, hippocampal and memory shrinkage are **not** inevitable. (It doesn't have to happen!) Recent studies have revealed that *new* growth in brain cells—or neurogenesis—is enhanced under the influence of a protein known as BDNF. This is produced is animals when they get aerobic exercise. And now we have evidence that the same thing happens in humans. This exercise can be any physical activity that makes you sweat, causes you to breathe harder, and gets your heart beating faster than at rest. This includes walking, stomping your feet to a wild beat, twirling, great sex. The idea is to get your body moving to feed your brain. Another study has indicated that DHA (an Omega-3 fat) has been shown to turn on the BDNF production. You can treat yourself to oysters and caviar if you choose or find a vegan nut or oil selection. If you choose a daily supplement, consider refrigerating the container after it's been opened because other factors such as light exposure and warm temperature can further accelerate the oxidation process and makes the supplement less effective.

What Does it All Mean?

Clearly, what we put into our body has a huge impact on the health and wellness of our incredible mind. We know this about our choice in food, exercise, oxygen, minerals and the actions we choose to take. An idea that is just as crucial, with devastating effects if used foolishly or in ignorance, is the power of the words we speak. The power of speech is undeniable. It is using your voice to share opinions and views, describe a past memory, and recite a poem. We can persuade others in our arguments into doing what we think is right, or what we think is better, or stop them from doing something we think is foolish.

We have a great responsibility when it comes to what we say to ourselves, about ourselves. What we say shows how we think. Negatives phrases cause damage. I've shared how damaged I felt being labeled as "rotten & miserable" by my father during my childhood. It took years to overcome and heal. Today it is common to hear people things like "I can't be bothered" or "Why does this happen to me?" Both infer a lack of control over your own life at the moment. And if you are not in control, who is? Is it funny to refer to a pause in a conversation as a "senior moment" or to someone changing their mind as "acting bipolar?" Do you ever overhear someone who is clearly stressed say "You are giving me a migraine" or refer to a co-worker as a real "pain in the neck" only to begin to rub their neck or shoulder at the same time? Our choice of words brings consequences.

Recent published researched looked into the topic of Social Cognitive and Affective Neuroscience. Essentially, they used MRI imaging machines to look at the changes in the brain when affirmations are used. Affirmations are positive statements that can help you challenge and overcome self-sabotaging and negative thoughts. The idea is that practicing self-affirmation actually activates the reward -or pleasure – center in your brain. This reward center is the same area that responds to other pleasurable experiences, like winning a big prize or eating your favorite foods. These reward circuits can also work to decrease pain and help maintain balance when you are under stress.

Knowing the benefits, I don't see any downside to saying affirmations on a daily basis.

There are a few ways I have learned to make them more powerful.

Keep the phrases short and simple. You want something that you can say any time and any place you want to remind yourself of these power words.

Stay in the present tense. Focus on the now, not what can happen in the future.

It makes sense. Use your own words, your own desires, and your own life.

This is the affirmation I have lived with for the past few decades. I have repeated it so often the words now live in my soul. I share it with you as a way to get started and invite you to use it, modify it, change it around and personalize it.

"I am a Magnificent Woman. I have an incredible mind. I have a strong, sexy, healthy body. I have a warm and loving heart. Something good will happen through me today."

There is no set length for an affirmation. I like descriptive adjectives so that's what I tend to use. Find words that describe the life you deserve. Say the affirmations out loud into a mirror in the morning, and again at night. And anytime in-between when you want to hear them again. Some topics are

Abundance:

I have all the money I need today.

My income exceeds my expenses.

I am blessed by the Universe with everything that I need.

I am rich by doing what I am passionate about.

Health:

I am active and full of energy.

I love my healthy body.

I choose to be healthy in every cell of my body.

I nourish my body with healthy choices.

Love:

I am loved.

I am confident and full of joy.

I am part of a loving fulfilling relationship.

I am grateful for the lover in my life.

Self-Appreciation:

I am worthy of great love in every area of my life.

I am confident, smart and capable.

My body is sacred and worthy of care.

I attract wonderful things into my life.

We choose who we are. We really do. The affirmations we choose to speak are a great way to reprogram the mind and visualize the life of our dreams. Affirming helps strengthen the beliefs that we hold inside whether they're positive or negative, so choose positive affirmations and reprogram your mind to believe in yourself. Remember thoughts, feeling, and actions all have power. Positive affirmations lead to positive feelings, which lead to positive actions, which will lead to a positive life.

Part 3

The Strong Sexy Healthy Body

The human body comes in all shapes and sizes, all different colors and hues. And just like the brain, we have an amazing amount of influence over what we do with our body to keep it running smoothly and efficiently. There are a few areas that I want to pay particular attention to here. These are parts of our bodies that we either take for granted or tend to ignore completely. I've talked with some people who still don't know how their own body works. Understanding your body, and how to help it run efficiently and use what Nature gives us to keep us strong and healthy only works in our favor.

Bones & Joints – Keeping us Moving

Our skeletal system is the foundation of the body and provides the central framework. It is what we are given – we cannot change it. This includes the bones and joints, giving us structure and allowing for movement. It is crucial that we understand how to care for our joints to avoid pain and weakness. Our joints rely on cartilage – connective tissue – to provide cushion and keep them from rubbing together. While cartilage is very beneficial to the body, it does have a drawback: it doesn't heal itself as well as most other soft tissues. The cartilage cells known as *chondrocytes* do not often replicate or repair themselves, which means damaged or injured cartilage will not likely heal well without medical intervention.

The degeneration of this cartilage may lead to arthritis and result in prolonged inflammation of your joints. **Arthritis** is a disease that affects the joints, causing severe pain and stiffness while reducing mobility. This can occur in almost any joint in the body and often affects weight bearing joints like the knees, hips, neck and lower back when the smooth cartilage begins to wear away. There are some steps we can take to prevent this from happening, including balance and flexibility exercises like yoga or Tai chi. Start with simple stretches and follow the instructions and signals from your own body. You may want to start to take steps to alleviate inflammation of the joints whenever possible, even before you see signs of swelling.

A natural remedy for the pain and swelling from arthritis is the spice *turmeric*. It is the flowering plant from the ginger family native to the Indian continent and popular in many Asian cuisines. Its bright golden yellow color is due to curcumin, the bioactive compound with anti-inflammatory and antioxidant properties. Turmeric has been used medicinally for more than 4000 years, and can easily be added to foods, teas or as a spice. Personally, I have used the powder, mixed with water applied directly on to a swollen joint. Once dried, rinse off. Be prepared to do this over a sink since the bright yellow orange color will drip and likely leave a trail.

Another herb that helps reduce inflammation is *Boswellia*. Boswellia serrata is a plant that produces Indian frankincense. The plant is native to much of India and the Punjab region that extends into Pakistan. The resin is extracted from the bark of the tree and was initially discovered after elephants rubbing the residue and eating the plant were calmer and healthier, so local healers began to study the various benefits of the entire plant system. (The things we learn from elephants!) It is an effective anti-inflammatory and pain killer that may prevent the loss of cartilage. Some research studies are looking at traditional uses of the plant being used to improve learning and memory while improving cognitive function. Other world studies are researching possible anticancer effects of boswellic acids. Currently this supplement can be taken as a tablet or in powder form, Boswellia serrata extract can also be added to baking or mixed into food. Boswellia cream is readily available and often used as a topical treatment for arthritis and to relieve muscle aches and pains. No wonder frankincense was believed to be one of the gifts of the magi!

Respiratory System - Keeping Us Breathing

Our respiratory system is what allows us to breathe. We NEED to breathe. And the easier it is for us to breathe, the easier it is for us to function. This system is divided into an upper and lower respiratory tract. The upper tract is the nose, throat and sinuses. Often, this area gets congested and requires immediate attention and treatment. The congestion could be a result of a common cold, allergies, stress or numerous other factors. Keeping this area clean and free from contamination is vital, as many have learned during the global spread of recent viral infections. One simple way to stay ahead is to be hydrated (always). Drinking lots of water and having the nasal passages moist keeps the mucus thin and loose and easier to expel. Consider adding garlic to your daily regimen in whatever quantities please your palate. Long considered to be

Nature's antibiotic, garlic contains allicin, which also has antiviral and antifungal properties. The cloves lessen inflammation while shrinking enlarged nasal passages due to any infection. Historically, garlic was prescribed for a number of conditions and illnesses, including respiratory problems, digestive issues and treating fatigue. Some writings indicate that the original Olympic athletes in ancient Greece were given garlic for it's possible "performance enhancing" agent used in sporting events! Today, garlic is used for conditions linked to the blood system and heart disease, and by some for prevention of a variety of cancers. It is linked to research in lowering osteoarthritis and protecting the heart during cardiac surgery. Although there is some very recent research that suggests that raw garlic has the most benefits, other studies show that both raw and cooked varieties are beneficial, or if you do not care for the taste, you can take the odorless capsules. The choice is yours.

The lower respiratory tract is essentially made up of our windpipe, the lungs and the diaphragm. The windpipe – trachea – has one main purpose: to conduct air into our lungs. It is tube shaped, about four inches long, and widens and lengthens with each breath in, then returns to its resting size with each breath out. The lungs are a pair of spongy air-filled organs located on either side of the chest and are two different sizes. The right lung is bigger while the left is smaller and still makes room for the heart. The lungs work with the heart to bring oxygen to the entire body. The diaphragm is the dome shaped muscle just below the lungs. When you inhale, the diaphragm lowers and the lungs expand to take in air. When you exhale and breathe out, it goes back to its original position. All you need to do is breathe in and out, your lungs do all the work. We can try and keep the surrounding environment as clean and healthy as possible by not smoking and staying away from secondhand smoke and limiting exposure to polluted settings. When we control our breathing we calm our nervous system, sending a signal to the brain that "all is well". This reduces stress, increases alertness and boosts the immune system. For centuries, yoga practitioners have used controlled breathing to promote concentration and improve vitality. Science is showing evidence of studies showing these practices help reduce symptoms associated with anxiety, insomnia, depression, attention deficit disorder and even PTSD. An easy exercise to calm and control your breathing is called the four – six method. Breathing through the diaphragm feels like pushing out the lower belly, as opposed to expanding the top of the chest. If you place your hands below your navel you will get a sense of where this is in your center of balance. Get in a comfortable position. Breathe in deeply through your nose to the count of four. Swallow. Slowly breathe out through your nose to the count of six. Try not to rush. Don't worry if you start to yawn, think of it as your lungs stretching out. Repeat this a few times until you feel completely relaxed.

To avoid contagious colds and infections you can have eucalyptus in your home year-round. The eucalyptus is actually a tree and the leaves, branches, roots and oils have been used medicinally for ages against bacteria and various fungi. Eucalyptus works as an expectorant by cleansing and draining mucus from the lungs, thinning the mucus, and lubricating the affected area of the respiratory tract. The oil from the leaves is anti-irritant and able to reduce redness and swelling, while strengthening the immune system with antioxidant properties. It is a natural decongestant, narrowing the blood vessels in the nose which decreases swelling and lets mucus drain and air flow freely. This is why you often see eucalyptus as the main ingredient for nasal sprays or throat lozenges during cold season. For centuries in Australia and Papua New Guinea the plant was used as medicine and food. As an antiseptic, it was used in wound care to prevent infection. The oil works as a stimulant to enhance brain performance, treat stress and revive drowsiness. As an anti-inflammatory, it's been useful to treat muscle and joint aches and pains, aid in dental and gum care and reduce body temperature in breaking a fever. You can keep it as a live plant, dried leaves for tea or essential oil to use a drop or two at a time.

Digestive System - Keeping Us Nourished

The digestive tract is probably the most complex system in the human body. In very, very simple terms, our digestive system is made up of the alimentary canal, which is commonly called the digestive tract. It is about thirty feet long from the mouth to the anus. There is an upper and lower tract. The upper GI (gastrointestinal) tract is essentially mechanical in function: it breaks down the food we consume. The lower GI tract is chemical, extracting the nutrients from that food and eliminating what we don't need.

The upper GI tract begins with the mouth when we taste our food. Food travels down the esophagus to the stomach, which holds the food while it's being processed. Generally speaking, it can take two to four hours for food to move from your stomach to your small intestine. Give yourself time to feel full and absorb that food! The stomach then uses rhythmic churning and grinding motions along with acid and enzymes to break down the food. Eating too fast can increase the possibility of overeating and increased risk of weight gain. Eating fast causes bigger glucose fluctuations, which can lead to insulin resistance. It has also been linked to erosive gastritis; an inflammation that eats away at the lining of the stomach that can lead to deep ulcers. Ulcers are open sores on the lining the stomach, causing a burning sensation in the abdomen resulting in pain, indigestion or nausea. In addition to gastritis, too much medication over a long period of time (including ibuprofen and aspirin) can contribute to ulcers or when medication is taken in high doses. (Consult your own expert resources and do your research).

The lower GI tract contains the small intestine and the large intestine, which is called the colon. It is in the small intestine that the "heavy duty" work of digestion really happens, and everything gets moved along. The liver and the pancreas assist the lower tract with the digestion of food to release nutrients. By the time food exits the body, it has been completely digested and almost all the nutrients have been absorbed into the bloodstream. The liver is the largest solid organ at almost three pounds and the only one that can regenerate. It cleanses the body of toxins, filters the blood and digests fats. The pancreas helps break down food by producing the hormone called insulin into the bloodstream, where it regulates the body's sugar level. Problems with insulin control can lead to diabetes. Diabetes is a well-known autoimmune disease where the beta cells in the pancreas are attacked and can no longer produce insulin. When there isn't enough insulin, too much blood sugar stays in your bloodstream. Over time this can cause health problems like heart disease, vision loss and kidney disease. Many studies show that being overweight, not getting any regular physical exercise, not getting enough sleep and too much stress increase the risk of diabetes. Stress is linked to several digestive issues, including IBS (irritable bowel syndrome), indigestion, heartburn, peptic ulcers and colitis. Managing the stress and anxiety in your life is **crucial**. Another factor linked to diabetes is the unknown amount of sugar consumed in the diet, especially in processed foods. Part of being strong and healthy is taking an active part of what you put into your body. Processed foods contain preservatives and up to eight times more sugar, artificial ingredients, refined carbohydrates and trans-fats than raw foods. Be careful what you consume.

A natural remedy for the entire digestive tract to use at any time is ginger. We actually use the rhizome, or root of the ginger plant for medicinal and cooking purposes. Grown worldwide, ginger is a member of the same plant family as cardamom and turmeric. Originally thought to be from Southeast Asia, the plant was valued in China, Ancient Greece and the Middle East. It was known to help with motion sickness (and morning sickness) and nausea and a longtime favorite of sailors worldwide as it still is today. Its anti-inflammatory properties make it great for relieving pain and swelling in joints or for menstrual discomfort. Since it causes the body to sweat, ginger has been used to bring down a fever. It helps boost the immune system by breaking down toxic substances in the body's organs and having a cleansing effect on the lymphatic system. Ginger has proven blood sugar regulation benefits. The gingerol compounds help prevent infections. According to research, one of the significant reasons ginger reduces nausea and other digestive discomforts is because it's carminative, which means it relieves flatulence, gas and bloating, aiding absorption. Since the properties of ginger help the body absorb nutrients more efficiently, the digestive system works smoothly and without interruptions. Food moves through the body and we take what we need while eliminating the waste. Add ginger to your food, in a tea, as a dietary supplement, in ginger beer or ginger ale. A little bit grated off the root goes a long way!

Female Reproductive Organs - Keeping Us Aware

There seems to be no greater mystery in the western world than the understanding of female anatomy. This is not due to a lack of available information. Rather, there seems to be a vast amount of voluntary ignorance when it comes to acknowledging and caring for women's reproductive organs. For years, it was easier to remove the entire reproductive system of a female than to learn the cause of a possible infection or malady in another area of the anatomy that was causing a disturbance in her (lack of passive) behavior or health.

The female reproductive anatomy includes both external and internal structures. Unfortunately, even today in some areas of the world for cultural, religious or political reasons, some women have no knowledge of either. There is an external (outside of the body) and an internal (inside) structure.

Biologically the external function is twofold: to let in sperm and to protect against infection. The main parts include the "labia majora" which is Latin for large lips and the "labia minora" meaning small lips. If you haven't looked in a mirror, these both surround the opening to the vagina and protect the internal organs. The skin is very delicate and easily irritated. These "lips" or folds come in all shapes, sizes and colors. There is no big or small, right or wrong. It is all skin that you want to keep healthy. You should gently clean the entire area and moisturize daily when desired. Treat with care. Next to and slightly below the vaginal opening are two tiny pea-sized glands called Bartholin's glands, which secrete fluid to keep the entire area lubricated. Above the opening is the clitoris, the small sensitive protrusion that is biologically comparable to the penis in males. It is extremely sensitive, containing approximately 8000 nerve endings in the tip alone. The clitoris is made up of eighteen distinct parts, a mixture of erectile tissue, muscle and nerves. For centuries leaders in various cultures around the world have denied the physical existence of the clitoris and, being horrified by the concept of a female enjoying orgasm, have removed the organ surgically. This practice continues to this day. The key role of the clitoris in the female body is in sexual stimulation and pleasure.

The internal reproductive organs include the vagina, which is a canal that joins the cervix to the outside of the body. This is the birth canal. It is not the term for the entire female system. The uterus is the hollow organ that is home to a developing fetus. A canal through the cervix allows sperm to enter and menstrual blood to exit. The ovaries are small glands on both sides of the uterus, producing eggs and numerous hormones. The Fallopian tubes are attached to the upper part of the uterus where the egg travels from the ovaries to the uterus.

The biology itself sounds relatively simple until the introduction of hormones, which influence this area of the female body from the onset of puberty at first menstruation until post menopause when the body has stopped producing eggs. The key hormones are estrogen, progesterone, FSH (follicle stimulating hormone), and luteinizing hormones. All play a role in the entire ovulation, menstruation and pregnancy. Hormone levels are a delicate balance. That balance can easily be disturbed by stress, nutrition, illness or changes in the environment.

Whether it is painful cramps, hot flashes or PMS there are numerous repetitive issues that happen to us where we require relief and comfort every month. Indigenous women in North America and Canada used the root of the black cohosh plant to help regulate the reproductive system. The Iroquois used it externally to ease aching joints and applied to the abdomen to relieve pain. The Algonquin used it for women's monthly pain and also for kidney problems. The Delaware tribe used the chopped root in mixtures for a women's tonic prior to and immediately after childbirth. The Cherokee used it as a diuretic and to fight fatigue and tuberculosis. The plant today is used to reduce inflammation, ease menstrual and menopausal symptoms and eliminate abdominal spasms. It improves the health of the immune system, prevents mood swings and helps promote restful sleep. The active ingredients in black cohosh include serotonin-like compounds, as well as a component (fukinolic acid) that can mimic estrogen in the body. When estrogen levels drop in the body, as during menopause, symptoms like hot flashes, night sweats, fatigue and erratic mood swings occur. Serotonin, found in the brain and the intestines, helps regulate mood and an overall sense of well-being. In addition to relieving symptoms connected with menopause, the plant acts as an antispasmodic to prevent muscle spasms. It can inhibit cramps and pains related to muscle strain, injury or chronic nervous tension. It is a potent natural sedative and can help with a long, restful sleep. It is used to remedy insomnia, anxiety and stress disorders. Recent studies have shown that a paste made from the root is effective in treating snakebites, which is how the plant got the alternate name of black snakeroot (or maybe hearkening back to the original power of Eve?) You can take black cohosh as a tea, in a tincture, in a capsule or in a powder form.

The Power of Pleasure

Even though it isn't necessarily common conversation in science class, all female mammals have a clitoris, the highly sensitive organ linked with pleasure and orgasm in humans. In the human female the external size can vary, from one to 1.5 cm, roughly the size of a tiny pea. Most of the clitoris is internal and not visible. Inside the body it can be as long as five inches. In early fetal development, the penis and the clitoris start out the same. They form into the different sexual organs at about week nine of pregnancy. Just like the penis, blood rushes to the clitoris when aroused, causing it to swell and the tissues to become erect. This increased blood flow also causes the rest of the vulva to deepen in color too as the vagina also widens and deepens. There are more than 8,000 nerve endings in the external tip of the clitoris alone. This is more than double those found in the penis. The organ can swell by fifty percent up to 300 percent when engorged or approaching arousal. As far as we know about biology and anatomy, the clitoris is the only known body part with the sole purpose of pleasure.

Having the ability to reach orgasm and experience various levels of physical pleasure doesn't mean that every woman shares these intense physical reactions in the same way, or in some cases at all. For many women, the very idea of intimacy carries emotional, social, psychological, religious, or physical limitations that prevent understanding and feeling the power of pleasure. For some, there is a social stigma attached enjoying sex. Many are raised since childhood with the impossible dichotomy of "virgin vs whore". A "good girl" keeps her legs together, doesn't know the parts of her own anatomy and keeps an intact hymen until becoming the property of a husband – becoming Mr.'s property. Instead of learning how her own body functions, she is told that that she has "dirty, smelly" parts, that every month she is cursed, and in some cultures, she is still made to pay a sin offering for committing the disgusting sin of menstruating. Contrast this with the guilt associated with the image of the wanton woman who sexually aware. She becomes cast as the temptress, the promiscuous easy woman who isn't wanted or respected by any "decent" partner. What happened to the Goddess? Where does the multi-orgasmic life-affirming unapologetically sexual woman fit in? Where is the celebration of the female?

Close to ten percent of women interviewed in various studies report never having experienced an orgasm. Some attribute this to lack of emotional intimacy, embarrassment over required arousal time, cultural expectations or prior physical trauma. The reasons and explanations are as varied as the women discussing them. Negative emotions play a major part in the lack of orgasm, which in some leads to low self-esteem, confusion, shame or avoidance of sex altogether. Only 18-22% of women claim to reach orgasm through vaginal sex alone. This could be attributed to the location of the clitoris on their individual body, or any number of physical and psychological factors. But it makes one wonder why all the literature and cultural history pretends that a woman can achieve delight and orgasm after a touch or a kiss. Could all the romance paperbacks be exaggerated? Could it be that science still doesn't understand the complicated physiology behind female pleasure? Science cannot really explain the reasoning behind a female orgasm. It is not to bring sperm into the body quicker, as some thought for ages. It is not to assist in aiding pregnancy. No. It is about pleasure and the female being satisfied enough to stop a moment and be around the eager male. During those intense rhythmic contractions, a vast amount of oxytocin, dopamine and serotonin all flood the body to the brain and back again. From the 30+ erogenous zones reported in the female body, most of these become receptive during the physical act of orgasm. The heart rate elevates during orgasm, and blood pressure and breathing rate often accelerate. Both of these responses are labelled mild aerobic activity, and lead to a type of euphoria which creates a sense of contentment.

Many, many women (43%) report having multiple orgasms during a sexual sharing experience. Researchers have learned that the climax could last from 20 seconds to 2 minutes, stating that the difference has to do with how aroused or ready the body is and how intense the stimulation is during the experience. So why not enjoy the pleasure your body is created for? What prohibits us from enjoying sex and sexual release?

We have five basic physical human senses (not counting the Sixth Sense or Intuition). Celebrating the experience of these senses helps us connect with the delight of our own bodies and the world around us. We rely on smell, taste, hearing, touch and sight to interpret our environment and send signals to the brain. Why not surround ourselves with incredible fragrances? Decadent or exciting tastes? Lovely music and outrageous laughter? Why not have soft fabrics against our skin and indulge in more hugs? And keep our life full of vibrant color and beautiful pictures? This is a life of learning about pleasure, in every little way that we can enjoy it.

The Health of the Body

We have an amazing amount of control about what we put into our bodies. We know that smart eating is imperative. Every cell, organ and bit of tissue in the human body needs water just to function. We know we need to move and suffer when too much time is spent in a sedentary position. Even standing up for two minutes after an hour of sitting is beneficial to the body. We hear people complain about their body and their health status all the time. Some insist their body won't accept certain food groups. Some say they can't abide fresh fruit, or drink water without adding soda. I acknowledge that each individual body is unique. My challenge is to invite you to listen to your own body and come to an agreement about walking and living in health.

You don't have to do anything fancy. You can make an agreement with your physical body in front of a mirror, or during a ritual in a sacred circle. The idea is to get your physical body in alignment with your mind and your spirit about the plan to be healthy. Make a "contract" or sacred agreement with your body. Treat it with respect and take some time to think about what you want to say – what you are willing to offer and what you expect in return. Remember your words have power and intentions make a difference.

This is what I said: "I am a Spirit and I have a mind. I live in a body which I will treat as a Temple. I appreciate and respect this body. I agree to listen to the urges and nudges about consuming the food this body requires and thrives on. I agree to thoughtfully consider what I eat, when I eat and how much I eat. I will be at the right healthy weight for my shape and size. I will sleep when prompted and not push past the limits of exhaustion. I will follow the desire to move, to dance, to touch, to kiss, to hug and to celebrate. "

Modify and adjust your agreement until it is right for you. You can add different terms and expectations. Include your body in your health decisions. You may be amazed at the outcome.

PART 4

The Warm & Loving Heart

Caring, compassion, communication and choices.

When we speak about having a "loving heart" in the common vernacular, we mean more than the physical organ inside the chest. That wonderful one-pound organ that beats about 115,000 times a day and pumps nearly 2000 gallons of blood. While vital to our physical life, we are so much more than an assembly of "parts." We are souls with the capacity to love, thrive, give, receive and believe. We are souls who live in a body which we can treat as a sacred temple. The "loving heart" is symbolic of the energy we give outward, that part of us we choose to share with the rest of the world. The Dalai Lama, a spiritual leader of millions of people and head monk and temporal leader of Tibetan Buddhism, teaches that "Happiness is a choice" which can be consciously made at the beginning of every single day. By stating this, he reminds people to take a proactive part in the kind of energy being shared, choosing to be positive and responsible for our own purpose and actions.

What makes someone warm and loving? Is it all instinct? Is it natural, expected behavior that humans have evolved? If so, why isn't everyone this way? Why do some choose to be cold and calculating or selfish? Is it the nature - nurture dispute around behavioral psychology? The "Nature-Nurture" debate has been discussed for ages, since before the Greek philosopher Hippocrates was alive and writing opinions. The "nature" side refers to who we are as human beings, how we are made up biologically and genetically. Then looking at "nurture," (nurturing, caring for, encouraging) examines the influence of learning and the environment, how we are influenced by what -and who - is around us. Most successful human behaviors are thought to be a combination of both traits. So, do we actively choose to be affectionate and loving or have we learned this behavior as being evolutionarily advantageous? It may not matter at all, as long as we know we have a choice.

We can choose to be a caring individual, one who is moved by the misery or unhappiness or joy of others. This reminds us that we as humans are all part of a "whole" – all one race. We also can choose to accept the self as an individual and the need for self-awareness and self-actualization, which was often historically considered to be "non-feminine" and selfish and therefore a negative trait. Both are important considerations. Both ways of looking at the world let us be caring people and let us feel with our emotions on a level that reaches out and accepts others as part of the same spiritual family.

Every major world religious (and many non-religious) tradition has some version of what is known as the "Golden Rule," treating others with the same kindness we wish for ourselves. Buddhist, Christian, Jain, Hindu, Islam, Jewish and Tao scholars all teach a variant of this philosophy. As we want others to respect our life and dignity, so we ought to respect and protect the life and dignity of others; as we want others to respect our freedoms of conscience, thought, and expression, so we must respect and defend these freedoms for others. This ethic of reciprocity, as it is sometimes called, is at the very heart of belief. This could point to our "true" essence: kindness, courage, passion and the virtues we associate with the best of being Human.

When we begin to care about the feelings and experiences of others, we begin to develop compassion. Being compassionate is different from being empathetic. Empathy and compassion are very different. They are represented in different areas of the brain. With empathy, we join the suffering of others who suffer, but stop short of actually helping. With compassion, we take a step away from the emotion of empathy and ask ourselves 'how can we help?' Remember our discussion of Quan-Yin?

Empathy is an important, primary emotion for human connection. It is the spark that can ignite compassion. But on its own, without compassion, empathy can also be harmful. As odd as this sounds, the reasoning is basically simple: Empathy is the brain's wired tendency to identify with those who are like us and close to us – close in proximity, close in familiarity, or close in relationship. And when we empathize with those close to us, those who are not close or are different become seen as being "other" and can seem threatening. It becomes a division of "us vs them." When left on its own without care and compassion, empathy can create more division than unity.

Empathy is considered a spontaneous and automatic part of our psychology which originates in the emotion centers of the brain. Empathetic feelings, thoughts, and decisions are generated mostly on an unconscious level, which means we are less aware and less intentional about those decisions, they just seem to "rise up" when needed.

Compassion is considered more reflective and deliberate, from the part of our psychology which originates in the cognitive, or reasoning, areas of the brain. Compassionate feelings, thoughts, and decisions pass through filters of consciousness. We take actions and make decisions.

Empathy is the tendency to join in others' suffering, but the focus is on those we perceive to be particularly close to us. So, empathy is limited. When it comes to helping those who could be considered to be "outsiders" who are suffering, our brains perceive it as real work, and tend to reject or put off the effort. While our instinct is to support and protect our own "family" group, we can perceive outsiders as part of an out group of "others" and a threat to our tiny social identity. Studies have found that empathy triggered from social connections makes it more likely that we will not be as protective or empathetic with individuals seen as belonging to this out group, or threatening tribe of outsiders. In its extreme, empathy can fuel aversion to those who are different from us. Someone who is truly different may actually damage the group by taking the care and assistance offered. (As if all resources are finite.)

Compassion is the joining in others' suffering, regardless of their social or personal identity. It is the perspective that in any person's suffering there is a common humanity – the recognition that no matter a person's cultural background, gender, sexual orientation, or age, we are like the other person in that very moment. Compassionate people lift themselves above their unconscious biases to see others in the environment with similar worth.

Though empathy can feel positive at first, it can also make you feel trapped. You are joining in other's suffering without taking any action to resolve or remedy the issue, so your empathy can simply be dwelling on or thinking about the problem. People prone to only empathetic responding may also be more likely to internalize symptoms mirroring depression from inaction. Compassion, on the other hand, is more constructive. It starts with empathy and then turns outward, with the intention being to help, to share, to be useful. The conscious choice is made to turn emotion into action. This triggers other positive outcomes: improved relationships, trust, and connections.

Feeling for another person's suffering is depleting and exhausting over time. When empathy is triggered in the face of another person's struggles, it can bring a relentless bombardment of negative emotions and experiences that, over time, can drain our intellectual resources and take a toll on our mental (and eventually physical) well-being.

Yet compassion is intentional and focused on a tangible solution. It centers on how to give and help another person. It is restorative versus draining. And, when we deliver that help, our brains receive a burst of dopamine, that lovely neurotransmitter delivering feelings of pleasure and reward. Helping feels good, and we are motivated to do it again in the future.

Having genuine compassion for others starts with having compassion for yourself. If you're overloaded and out of balance, it's impossible to help others find their balance.

Communication – How We Connect

We communicate by sending and receiving messages, ideas, images, and all sorts of information to the world around us. This includes other people, animals, plants, the space within, the space without, the seen and unseen. We use a variety of methods, including words, pictures, sound, space, and movement. Through these we are able to connect on a deep and meaningful level at any given moment of our lives.

There are certain words that carry power that can be used in a positive manner to make an impact in a conversation or change a mood. Research shows that people respond in a positive manner when they hear the sound of their name, even in a room full of noisy conversation. People in a deep coma in a hospital setting are more likely to respond to their name than any other word. Why is this? Do we imagine we are being called home? The "Feel good" hormones like dopamine and serotonin are released into your brain when your ears encode that your name has just been said aloud. This burst of excitement makes people happy and sends an unconscious signal similar to trust to the brain. This creates a type of energy force. Some MRI research has examined brain activation patterns in response to patients hearing their own names versus other names. Findings showed several regions in the left hemisphere experienced greater activation to one's own name. Does this indicate a level of pleasure or reward? What other words might elicit such powerful positive responses? How about words such as: Love, Beauty, Yes, Wondrous, Radiant, Splendid. My own favorite: Magnificent. Using these types of words to describe and encourage people and situations help build positive energy all around us. Perhaps we should increase usage in our own vocabulary.

We also connect through sound. Even something as basic as a rattle or a hum can be the beginning of music. The drum has been played as a musical instrument for more than 7700 years in recorded history, mimicking the beat of the human heart. Music has been called the Universal Language, the powerful healer and the connection with Nature and the Divine. Science now suggests that music can have a profound effect on individuals – from helping improve the recovery of motor and cognitive function in stroke patients, reducing symptoms of depression in patients suffering from dementia, even helping patients undergoing surgery to experience less pain and heal faster. We use it to soothe as much as to inspire.

Sound is measured in frequency and amplitude. Amplitude refers to how forceful the sound wave is. Frequency measures the number of sound waves per second. The unit for frequency is the hertz (Hz) and the range for humans is from 20 to 20,000 Hz. The average frequency range for human speech varies from 80 to 260 Hz. The human ear can detect a tremendously wide range of frequencies, from the low rumbles of a distant elephant call (up to six miles away!) to the high-pitched whistle of a flying mosquito. Sound is known to influence human brain function. Audio stimulation not only affects the hearing system and the vestibular (balance) system, but it also activates the brain areas associated with emotional processing and higher mental processes. Music and sound therapy have been studied with results focused on improving physical and mental health. How does sound frequency interact with our spiritual health? Does it touch our very soul?

Researchers in the field of sound and frequencies report that tones used in ancient sacred music at about 174 Hz are associated with a reduction of pain and stress. It's the lowest tone in the intonation "Solfeggio scale", a series of six ascending notes that were sung by Gregorian monks to bring spiritual blessings and harmony.

At 285 Hz the sound is thought to activate the body into cellular regeneration encouraging healing from cuts, burns or other injuries. The frequency of 432 Hz is supposed to lead to greater levels of emotional and mental clarity. This particular tuning is considered optimal for opera singers. Music that's tuned to 440 Hz is considered "cerebral" music, pushing even further in cognitive development. This tone historically was thought to activate the "Third Eye" energy area in the human body. Tuning music at 528 Hz is described as the "miracle" (or "Mi" on the scale) transformation sound, associated with blessings and increased creativity. Music played at 639 Hz affects the heart area and is used in therapy to produce positive feelings. This sound is identified as a social frequency, one of understanding, sympathy, tolerance, and mutual respect. Sound therapy at 852 Hz produces a tone that's associated with redirecting the mind's focus away from negative patterns and helps alleviate depression and anxiety.

The 963 Hz frequencies have become associated with the pineal gland (behind the Third Eye area and linked to the central nervous system) and thought to activate a sense of higher spiritual development.

From seeking security and comfort, to healing the body to stretching our soul, the music we choose to listen to plays a big part in influencing our daily decisions and channeling our energy focus. We can decide at any given moment what frequency we select to communicate with our internal body and our external world.

The choices we make identify who we choose to be at any given moment. We regularly choose what information to let into our conscious being, from social media to music to the voices of those we love. We choose what nutrients to put in our body, how to hydrate the body, what colors appeal to us and how we move. Of all the choices we make over a lifetime, there are a few important ones that keep influencing the majority of our results. The first is to choose to Love Yourself. Take your life seriously and treat it with respect. When we love and honor ourselves, we tend to be more generous in how we love and honor others. Second in importance and not to be ignored is to choose the people around you. Whether friends or lovers we find happiness and value in those closest to us.

As we grow and change, the level of interactions with those closest to us grow and develop as well. Consider the three psychological developmental phases of a woman's life and how the needs and opportunities change with each one. These are commonly referred to as "Mother/Maiden/Crone" for the three separate stages of maturity and growth.

As the Maiden, a young woman is experimenting with newfound independence and freedom, making decisions that influence the direction of her future. She is sampling life and trying on new relationships. Others in the immediate social circle will be experiencing similar opportunities, but there is still room and a need for wiser mentors and teachers. Due to changing social roles and contemporary definitions, this period of autonomy can now continue to extend for several decades.

The phase known as the Mother arrives when something other than the individual takes on the utmost importance. While traditionally associated with childbearing, this could also refer to a committed partnership, a career, or the discovery of a passion that demands all energy and attention. During this time there is a growth in maturity as commitments are honored and relationships and dependents are nurtured. This demands more effort and devotion than the Maiden stage, and there becomes a need to be – and stay – centered and grounded in order to stay completely involved.

The Crone is the most mysterious time of all. This is the time when a woman stops producing eggs which can bring forth human life. When egg production ceases, the need for bleeding, or cleansing, also ceases. Yet production of creativity, interest and curiosity continues. Common folklore and even fairy tales have described a woman in this time of her life as old, a hag, a crone and even as an evil life-sucking witch. Looking at the word “hag”, some historians have thought it to be associated with the Old Norse term “hogg” or “hagge”, which originally referred to the bog, a geographical wetland describing dark, muddy ground that looked like dead plants. Any people associated with this type of terrain would have been well outside the accepted social circle, and considered frightening to young children. So the connection between a dark gloomy remote place with an older isolated outsider became an accepted symbol of fear and loathing. The “hag” or the “bogeyman” was out to get you if you wandered from the safety of the tribe, and this persona was the inevitable fate of any woman who grew old, alone and past her child-bearing or life bearing years.

Yet there is another way to examine this word. Consider the ancient Greek term "hagia". Its proper usage meant to be 'held in awe', to be seen with reverence. The word was used in biblical times to refer to consecrated items or symbols. Today, the architectural monument in Istanbul, Turkey known as the Hagia Sofia stands as a marvel that has inspired visitors for more than 1500 years. Thought by some scholars to be built on the site of an Etruscan pagan temple, this grand building became a church in the 6th century CE, then converted into a mosque after the Ottoman conquest. The name remains the same: Hagia meaning Holy and Sofia, the ancient Greek word for wisdom. Holy Wisdom. Not a scary evil dark old woman in a bog.

The word crone has recently been poetically associated with "crown" or the top of the head. The meaning found in common dictionaries is quite different. We find words like "withered, used, old, ugly" that symbolize the lack of fullness and vitality. It was understood by the common folk that once a woman reached the age of menopause she would become dry and withered. She could no longer produce life. She no longer bled every month. She had outlived her primary purpose. Yet what actually happens is largely a function of hormones, not a person's usefulness in life. Fertility is affected, not creativity. Not the ability to teach, nurture, love, heal, protect or craft. Dr. Jean Shinoda Bolen, the Jungian psychoanalyst and best-selling author has identified the energy and potential of this phase as the "Juicy Crone", one far removed from the withered and lifeless villain of the patriarchal fairy tale. In her teachings, she exhorts crones to embrace their passion and new possibilities. In describing the need to build a social circle of like-minded individuals and avoid becoming isolated or ignored, she describes the WiseWoman circle in her book "Goddesses in Older Women".

"To transform a group that you already have into a WiseWoman circle or create a new one the first consideration are the members, who will the circle be? Are they "juicy crones?

Does each woman have wisdom and compassion, a sense of humor, a great laugh, Spirit and soul?

Is she outraged at injustice and indifference?

Does she want to make a difference?

Does she have a sense of community, faith that there is meaning in life and that it maters what we do?

Does she care about the wellbeing of others beyond her own, for values that are lost, for the survival of a neighborhood or the planet?

Can you count on her?"

All this and more go on to describe how we search out each other when we reach different stages in our lives. We make conscious decisions every day. We can also make important spiritual decisions every day. Why not decide we are worthy of the very best?

Afterword

When we become confident in who we really are, we tend to vibrate at a higher level. We attract what we send out. At the very beginning of this book I shared my personal mantra – my philosophy (from the word Sophia, or wisdom!) with you. Perhaps now it makes a bit more sense. I invite you to join me and use it as your own. Modify it, improve it, and personalize it. But join me. Together we make a difference. We can care about each other and create a community of vitality and true magnificence. Here it is again so you don't have to go back to the front page:

I am a Magnificent Woman we know the Goddess Archetypes now, and can call on any one of them as needed

I have an Incredible Mind with good nutrition, good vibrations and good words

I have a strong sexy healthy body we move, we breathe, we eat, we enjoy

I have a warm and loving heart that cares, has compassion, communicates and makes wise choices

Something GOOD will happen through me today! I know it.

Thank you for sharing this journey with me.

I will share my “things you just have to do” list below, and the sacred covenant I made with my body to be living in health.

May your journey Be Magnificent!

www.ingramcontent.com/pod-product-compliance
Lightning Source LLC
LaVergne TN
LVHW050553160826
845677LV00011B/2300

* 9 7 9 8 3 7 0 3 2 7 3 0 8 *